Healing S... Bro...

Experience Emotional Healing And Healing The Wounds Of The Past

By

Chris Adkins

Visit Blog

http://www.livingabrightlifenow.com

Disclaimer Of Warranty / Limitations Of Liability

The author and publisher of this book and the accompanying materials have used their best efforts to accurately represent this product and its potential in preparing this book/program. The author and publisher make no representation or warranties with respect to the accuracy, applicability, fitness, or completeness of the contents of this book/program. The information contained in this book is strictly for informational and/or educational purposes and should serve only as a general guide and not as the ultimate source of subject information. The author and publisher shall in no event be held liable or responsible to any person, party, or entity regarding any direct, indirect, punitive, special, incidental or other consequential damages or loss arising directly or indirectly from any use of this material, and without warranties. *I am not a lawyer*. This information is provided and sold with the knowledge that the author and publisher do not offer any legal or other professional advice. As always, if you have any specific questions, the advice of a competent legal, tax, accounting, financial, medical, or other appropriately qualified professional should be sought. The author and publisher do not warrant the performance, effectiveness or applicability of any sites listed or linked to in this book or any accompanying materials. All links are for information purposes only and are not warranted for content, accuracy or any other implied or explicit purpose.

Copyright © 2014 by Chris Adkins

All rights reserved. No material in this book may be reproduced, transmitted, or utilized in any form or by any means, electronic or mechanical, including photocopying, recording, or by any information storage and retrieval system, without permission from the author.

About The Author – Chris Adkins

Inventor and Author, Formal Education - Psychology

Specializing in helping individuals experience joy, wholeness and healing, peace of mind, and comfort for the spirit, soul, and body.

With past health challenges and questions, this began her quest to find answers. Her journey has led to an exhaustive study of bible scripture and self-help, seeking the 'genuine truth' and not just opinions or suggestions disguised as truth. She had found that the scripture is the inspired word of God, which led her to the scripture 'I am the way and the truth and the life' (John 14:6). She enjoys a tranquil peace now, and knows where to seek to maintain her comfort, health and peace of mind.

The Author's Mission:

My mission in life is not merely to survive, but to thrive; and to do so with some passion, some compassion, some humor and some style. - Dr. Maya Angelou

Table Of Contents

Disclaimer Of Warranty/Limitations Of Liability

About The Author – Chris Adkins

Introduction

Chapter 1 – Healing Scriptures For A Broken Heart

Conclusion

Check Out My Other Books On Amazon

Introduction

Hello, Chris Adkins here and I offer you a warm welcome and thank you for your interest in this book. Emotions can play havoc in our lives at times whether suffering the loss of a family member, a bad break-up, children leaving the nest, or any other of the too many opportunities for our emotions to carry us away. We are emotional beings period. The movie industry and advertisers know emotion sells. Although all these emotions are perfectly healthy and normal, when certain emotions begin to control our thoughts and have negative effects on our body, we often need help to get through these rough times.

God said, "I AM the Lord that heals you." Jesus said in Luke chapter four that He came to heal the broken hearted. Jesus also tells us He is familiar with the weaknesses, pain and suffering that we go through. He has provided for us His Word that gives us comfort, hope and peace. Read through the scriptures taking them to heart and you will experience the peace of mind that Jesus has for us when He said, "my peace I give you". Be comforted and encouraged, experience God's peace!

Make sure to read the entire book.

Enjoy!

Chris Adkins

Chapter 1 – Healing Scriptures For A Broken Heart

1 THE SPIRIT of the Lord God is upon me, because the Lord has anointed and qualified me to preach the Gospel of good tidings to the meek, the poor, and afflicted; He has sent me to bind up and heal the brokenhearted, to proclaim liberty to the [physical and spiritual] captives and the opening of the prison and of the eyes to those who are bound, [Romans 10:15]

2 To proclaim the acceptable year of the Lord [the year of His favor] and the day of vengeance of our God, to comfort all who mourn, [Matthew 11:2-6; Luke 4:18-19; Luke 7:22]

3 To grant [consolation and joy] to those who mourn in Zion–to give them an ornament (a garland or diadem) of beauty instead of ashes, the oil of joy instead of mourning, the garment [expressive] of praise instead of a heavy, burdened, and failing spirit–that they may be called oaks of righteousness [lofty, strong, and magnificent, distinguished for uprightness, justice, and right standing with God],

the planting of the Lord, that He may be glorified.

ISAIAH 61:1-3 – LUKE 4:18-19
(Amplified Bible)

Instead of your shame you will receive a double portion, and instead of disgrace you will rejoice in your inheritance. And so you will inherit a double portion in your land, and everlasting joy will be yours.

ISAIAH 61:7
(New International Version)

For I will restore health to you, And I will heal your wounds, says the Lord...

JEREMIAH 30:17
(Amplified Bible)

The crooked places shall be made straight, and the rough roads shall be made smooth...

LUKE 3:4-6
(Amplified Bible)

They who sow in tears shall reap in joy and singing.

PSALM 126:5
(Amplified Bible)

You keep track of all my sorrows. You have collected all my tears in your bottle. You have recorded each one in your book.

PSALM 56:8
(New Living Translation)

I have heard your prayer, I have seen your tears …

ISAIAH 38:5
(Amplified Bible)

God, Who comforts and encourages and refreshes and cheers the depressed and the sinking

2 CORINTHIANS 7:6

(Amplified Bible)

Blessed and enviably happy [with a happiness produced by the experience of God's favor and especially conditioned by the revelation of His matchless grace] are those who mourn, for they shall be comforted! [Isaiah 61:2]

MATTHEW 5:4
(Amplified Bible)

"This is the rest with which you may cause the weary to rest," and, "This is the refreshing"

ISAIAH 28:11-12
(New King James Version)

16 And I will ask the Father, and He will give you another Comforter (Counselor, Helper, Intercessor, Advocate, Strengthener, and Standby), that He may remain with you forever—

17 The Spirit of Truth, Whom the world cannot

receive (welcome, take to its heart), because it does not see Him or know and recognize Him. But you know and recognize Him, for He lives with you [constantly] and will be in you.

18 I will not leave you as orphans [comfortless, desolate, bereaved, forlorn, helpless]; I will come [back] to you.

JOHN 14:16-18
(Amplified Bible)

16 Now may our Lord Jesus Christ Himself and God our Father, Who loved us and gave us everlasting consolation and encouragement and well-founded hope through [His] grace (unmerited favor),

17 Comfort and encourage your hearts and strengthen them [make them steadfast and keep them unswerving] in every good work and word.

2 THESSALONIANS 2:16-17
(Amplified Bible)

I, even I, am He who comforts you

ISAIAH 51:12
(Amplified Bible)

1 The Lord is my Shepherd [to feed, guide, and shield me], I shall not lack.

2 He makes me lie down in [fresh, tender] green pastures; He leads me beside the still and restful waters. [Revelation 7:17]

3 He refreshes and restores my life (my self); He leads me in the paths of righteousness [uprightness and right standing with Him—not for my earning it, but] for His name's sake.

4 Yes, though I walk through the [deep, sunless] valley of the shadow of death, I will fear or dread no evil, for You are with me; Your rod [to protect] and Your staff [to guide], they comfort me.

5 You prepare a table before me in the presence of my enemies. You anoint my head with oil; my

[brimming] cup runs over.

6 Surely or only goodness, mercy, and unfailing love shall follow me all the days of my life, and through the length of my days the house of the Lord [and His presence] shall be my dwelling place.

PSALM 23:1-6
(Amplified Bible)

26 But the Comforter (Counselor, Helper, Intercessor, Advocate, Strengthener, Standby), the Holy Spirit, Whom the Father will send in my name [in My place, to represent Me and act on My behalf], He will teach you all things. And He will cause you to recall (will remind you of, bring to your remembrance) everything I have told you.

27 Peace I leave with you; My [own] peace I now give and bequeath to you. Not as the world gives do I give to you. Do not let your hearts be troubled, neither let them be afraid. [Stop allowing yourselves to be agitated and disturbed; and do not permit yourselves to be fearful and intimidated and cowardly and unsettled.]

JOHN 14:26-27
(Amplified Bible)

1 I will exalt you, Lord, for you lifted me out of the depths
and did not let my enemies gloat over me.

2 Lord my God, I called to you for help,
and you healed me.

3 You, Lord, brought me up from the realm of the dead;
you spared me from going down to the pit.

4 Sing the praises of the Lord, you his faithful people;
praise his holy name.

5 For his anger lasts only a moment, but his favor lasts a lifetime; weeping may stay for the night, but rejoicing comes in the morning.

6 When I felt secure, I said, "I will never be shaken."

7 Lord, when you favored me, you made my royal mountain stand firm; but when you hid your face, I

was dismayed.

8 To you, Lord, I called; to the Lord I cried for mercy:

9 "What is gained if I am silenced, if I go down to the pit? Will the dust praise you?
Will it proclaim your faithfulness?

10 Hear, Lord, and be merciful to me; Lord, be my help."

11 You turned my wailing into dancing; you removed my sackcloth and clothed me with joy,

12 that my heart may sing your praises and not be silent. Lord my God, I will praise you forever.

PSALM 30
(New International Version)

28 Do you not know? Have you not heard? The Lord is the everlasting God,
The Creator of the ends of the earth.
He will not grow tired or weary, and his understanding no one can fathom.

29 He gives strength to the weary and increases the power of the weak.

30 Even youths grow tired and weary,
and young men stumble and fall;

31 but those who hope in the Lord
will renew their strength.
They will soar on wings like eagles;
they will run and not grow weary,
they will walk and not be faint.

ISAIAH 40:28-31
(New International Version)

20 My child, pay attention to what I say.
Listen carefully to my words.

21 Don't lose sight of them. Let them penetrate deep into your heart,

22 for they bring life to those who find them, and healing to their whole body.

23 Guard your heart above all else,

for it determines the course of your life.

PROVERBS 4:20-23
(New Living Translation)

17 For our light affliction, which is for the moment, works for us more and more exceedingly an eternal weight of glory;

18 while we don't look at the things which are seen, but at the things which are not seen. For the things which are seen are temporal, but the things which are not seen are eternal.

2 CORINTHIANS 4:17-18
(World English Bible)

1 Therefore, we also, who have all of these witnesses who surround us like clouds, let us throw off from us all the weights of the sin which is always ready for us, and let us run with patience this race that is set for us.

2 And let us gaze at Yeshua, him who is The Author

and the perfecter of our faith, who for the joy that was his, endured the cross and ignored the shame, and he sits upon the right side of the throne of God.

HEBREWS 12:1-2
(Aramaic Bible in Plain English)

Why am I discouraged? Why is my heart so sad? I will put my hope in God! I will praise him again--my Savior and my God!

PSALM 42:11
(New Living Translation)

Those whom the LORD has ransomed will return; they will enter Zion with a happy shout. Unending joy will crown them, happiness and joy will overwhelm them; grief and suffering will disappear.

ISAIAH 51:11
(New English Translation Bible)

Cast your burden on the Lord [releasing the weight

of it] and He will sustain you; He will never allow the [consistently] righteous to be moved (made to slip, fall, or fail).
[1 Peter 5:7]

PSALM 55:22
(Amplified Bible)

Casting the whole of your care [all your anxieties, all your worries, all your concerns, once and for all] on Him, for He cares for you affectionately and cares about you watchfully. [Psalm 55:22]

1 PETER 5:7
(Amplified Bible)

For You have rescued my soul from death, My eyes from tears, My feet from stumbling.

PSALM 116:8
(New American Standard)

Be of good courage, and he shall strengthen your

heart, all you that hope in the LORD.

PSALM 31:24
(American King James Version)

For the Lamb on the throne will be their Shepherd. He will lead them to springs of life-giving water. And God will wipe every tear from their eyes.

REVELATION 7:17
(New Living Translation)

He will swallow up death forever. The Almighty LORD will wipe away tears from every face, and he will remove the disgrace of his people from the whole earth. The LORD has spoken.

ISAIAH 25:8
(God's Word Translation)

A cheerful heart is good medicine, but a broken spirit saps a person's strength.

PROVERBS 17:22
(New Living Translation)

A joyful heart makes a cheerful face, but with a heartache comes depression.

PROVERBS 15:13
(God's Word Translation)

Every day is a terrible day for a miserable person, but a cheerful heart has a continual feast.

PROVERBS 15:15
(God's Word Translation)

God will wipe away every tear from their eyes; and death shall be no more, neither shall there be anguish (sorrow and mourning) nor grief nor pain any more, for the old conditions and the former order of things have passed away. [Isaiah 25:8; Isaiah 35:10]

REVELATION 21:4

(Amplified Bible)

A Psalm. A cry out to God for help!

PSALM 77:1-20
(New Living Translation)

You comfort me and make me greater than ever.

PSALM 71:21
(God's Word Translation)

I will lie down and sleep peacefully, for you, LORD, make me safe and secure.

Psalm 4:8
(New English Translation Bible)

16 But now this is what the LORD says: "Do not weep any longer, for I will reward you," says the LORD. "Your children will come back to you from the distant land of the enemy.

17 There is hope for your future," says the LORD. "Your children will come again to their own land."

JEREMIAH 31:16-17
(New Living Translation)

Whatever happens, my dear brothers and sisters, rejoice in the Lord. I never get tired of telling you these things, and I do it to safeguard your faith.

PHILIPPIANS 3:1
(New Living Translation)

12 So then, brace up and reinvigorate and set right your slackened and weakened and drooping hands and strengthen your feeble and palsied and tottering knees, [Isaiah 35:3]

13 And cut through and make firm and plain and smooth, straight paths for your feet [yes, make them safe and upright and happy paths that go in the right direction], so that the lame and halting [limbs] may not be put out of joint, but rather may be cured.

HEBREWS 12:12-13
(Amplified Bible)

For this reason I remind you to fan into flame the gift of God, which is in you through the laying on of my hands.

2 TIMOTHY 1:6
(New International Version)

My comfort in my suffering is this: Your promise preserves my life.

PSALM 119:50
(New International Version)

3 Praise be to the God and Father of our Lord Jesus Christ, the Father of compassion and the God of all comfort,

4 who comforts us in all our troubles, so that we can comfort those in any trouble with the comfort we ourselves receive from God.

2 CORINTHIANS 1:3-4
(New International Version)

26 For the Lord shall be your confidence, firm and strong, and shall keep your foot from being caught [in a trap or some hidden danger].

27 Withhold not good from those to whom it is due [its rightful owners], when it is in the power of your hand to do it. [Romans 13:7; Galatians 6:10]

PROVERBS 3:26-27
(Amplified Bible)

The LORD gives strength to his people; the LORD blesses his people with peace.

PSALM 29:11
(New International Version)

3 With perfect peace you will protect those whose minds cannot be changed, because they trust you.

4 Trust the LORD always, because the LORD, the LORD alone, is an everlasting rock.

ISAIAH 26:3-4
(God's Word Translation)

6 For to us a Child is born, to us a Son is given; and the government shall be upon His shoulder, and His name shall be called Wonderful Counselor, Mighty God, Everlasting Father [of Eternity], Prince of Peace. [Isaiah 25:1; Isaiah 40:9-11; Matthew 28:18; Luke 2:11]

7 Of the increase of His government and of peace there shall be no end, upon the throne of David and over his kingdom, to establish it and to uphold it with justice and with righteousness from the [latter] time forth, even forevermore. The zeal of the Lord of hosts will perform this. [Daniel 2:44; 1 Corinthians 15:25-28; Hebrews 1:8]

ISAIAH 9:6-7
(Amplified Bible)

11 For I know what I have planned for you,' says the Lord. 'I have plans to prosper you, not to harm you. I have plans to give you a future filled with hope.

12 When you call out to me and come to me in prayer, I will hear your prayers.

13 When you seek me in prayer and worship, you will find me available to you. If you seek me with all your heart and soul, I will make myself available to you,' says the Lord.

JEREMIAH 29:11-13
(New English Translation Bible)

Call to Me and I will answer you and show you great and mighty things, fenced in and hidden, which you do not know (do not distinguish and recognize, have knowledge of and understand).

JEREMIAH 33:3
(Amplified Bible)

Again Jesus said, "Peace be with you! As the Father

has sent me, I am sending you."

JOHN 20:21
(New International Version)

17 When the righteous cry for help, the Lord hears, and delivers them out of all their distress and troubles.

18 The Lord is close to those who are of a broken heart and saves such as are crushed with sorrow for sin and are humbly and thoroughly penitent.

19 Many evils confront the [consistently] righteous, but the Lord delivers him out of them all.

PSALM 34:17-19
(Amplified Bible)

I have told you these things, so that in Me you may have [perfect] peace and confidence. In the world you have tribulation and trials and distress and frustration; but be of good cheer [take courage; be confident, certain, undaunted]! For I have overcome the world. [I have deprived it of power to harm you and have conquered it for you.]

JOHN 16:33
(Amplified Bible)

But the meek will inherit the land and enjoy peace and prosperity.

PSALM 37:11
(New International Version)

1 My child, never forget the things I have taught you. Store my commands in your heart.

2 If you do this, you will live many years, and your life will be satisfying.

3 Never let loyalty and kindness leave you! Tie them around your neck as a reminder. Write them deep within your heart.

4 Then you will find favor with both God and people, and you will earn a good reputation.

PROVERBS 3:1-4
(New Living Translation)

5 Trust in the LORD with all your heart; do not depend on your own understanding.

6 Seek his will in all you do, and he will show you which path to take.

7 Don't be impressed with your own wisdom. Instead, fear the LORD and turn away from evil.

8 Then you will have healing for your body and strength for your bones.

PROVERBS 3:5-8
(New Living Translation)

3 Strengthen the feeble hands, steady the knees that give way;

4 say to those with fearful hearts, "Be strong, do not fear;

your God will come,
He will come with vengeance; with divine retribution
he will come to save you."

5 Then will the eyes of the blind be opened
and the ears of the deaf unstopped.

6 Then will the lame leap like a deer, and the mute
tongue shout for joy. Water will gush forth in the
wilderness
and streams in the desert.

ISAIAH 35:3-6
(New International Version)

19 They cried out to the Lord in their distress;

He delivered them from their troubles.

20 He sent them an assuring word and healed them;
He rescued them from the pits where they were
trapped.

PSALM 107:19-20
(New English Translation Bible)

37 Yet amid all these things we are more than conquerors and gain a surpassing victory through Him Who loved us.

38 For I am persuaded beyond doubt (am sure) that neither death nor life, nor angels nor principalities, nor things impending and threatening nor things to come, nor powers,

39 Nor height nor depth, nor anything else in all creation will be able to separate us from the love of God which is in Christ Jesus our Lord.

ROMANS 8:37-39
(Amplified Bible)

He calmly ransomed my soul from the war waged against me, for there was a vast crowd who stood against me.

PSALM 55:18
(International Standard Version)

28 Then they cry to the Lord in their trouble, and He

brings them out of their distresses.

29 He hushes the storm to a calm and to a gentle whisper, so that the waves of the sea are still. [Psalm 89:9; Matthew 8:26]

30 Then the men are glad because of the calm, and He brings them to their desired haven.

31 Oh, that men would praise [and confess to] the Lord for His goodness and loving-kindness and His wonderful works to the children of men!

PSALM 107:28-31
(Amplified Bible)

No weapon forged to be used against you will succeed; you will refute everyone who tries to accuse you. This is what the LORD will do for his servants--I will vindicate them," says the LORD.

ISAIAH 54:17
(New English Translation Bible)

He heals the brokenhearted and binds up their wounds [curing their pains and their sorrows]. [Psalm 34:18; Isaiah 57:15; Isaiah 61:1; Luke 4:18]

PSALM 147:3
(Amplified Bible)

Great peace have they who love Your law; nothing shall offend them or make them stumble. [Proverbs 3:2; Isaiah 32:17]

PSALM 119:165
(Amplified Bible)

Pleasant words are honey from a honeycomb— sweet to the soul and healing for the body.

PROVERBS 16:24
(International Standard Version)

The words of the godly are a life-giving fountain; the words of the wicked conceal violent intentions.

PROVERBS 10:11
(New Living Translation)

A peaceful heart leads to a healthy body; jealousy is like cancer in the bones.

PROVERBS 14:30
(New Living Translation)

A gentle tongue [with its healing power] is a tree of life, but willful contrariness in it breaks down the spirit.

PROVERBS 15:4
(Amplified Bible)

The words of a [discreet and wise] man's mouth are like deep waters [plenteous and difficult to fathom], and the fountain of skillful and godly Wisdom is like a gushing stream [sparkling, fresh, pure, and life-giving].

PROVERBS 18:4

(Amplified Bible)

The strong spirit of a man sustains him in bodily pain or trouble, but a weak and broken spirit who can raise up or bear?

PROVERBS 18:14
(Amplified Bible)

10 Fear not [there is nothing to fear], for I am with you; do not look around you in terror and be dismayed, for I am your God. I will strengthen and harden you to difficulties, yes, I will help you; yes, I will hold you up and retain you with My [victorious] right hand of rightness and justice. [Acts 18:10]

11 Behold, all they who are enraged and inflamed against you shall be put to shame and confounded; they who strive against you shall be as nothing and shall perish.

12 You shall seek those who contend with you but shall not find them; they who war against you shall be as nothing, as nothing at all.

13 For I the Lord your God hold your right hand; I am the Lord, Who says to you, Fear not; I will help you!

ISAIAH 41:10-13
(Amplified Bible)

How beautiful upon the mountains are the feet of him who brings good news, who publishes peace, who brings good news of happiness, who publishes salvation, who says to Zion, "Your God reigns."

ISAIAH 52:7
(English Standard Version)

14 Stand therefore [hold your ground], having tightened the belt of truth around your loins and having put on the breastplate of integrity and of moral rectitude and right standing with God,

15 And having shod your feet in preparation [to face the enemy with the firm-footed stability, the promptness, and the readiness produced by the good news] of the Gospel of peace. [Isaiah 52:7]

EPHESIANS 6:14-15
(Amplified Bible)

3 He was despised and rejected and forsaken by men, a Man of sorrows and pains, and acquainted with grief and sickness; and like One from Whom men hide their faces He was despised, and we did not appreciate His worth or have any esteem for Him.

4 Surely He has borne our grief's (sicknesses, weaknesses, and distresses) and carried our sorrows and pains [of punishment], yet we [ignorantly] considered Him stricken, smitten, and afflicted by God [as if with leprosy].
[Matthew 8:17]

5 But He was wounded for our transgressions, He was bruised for our guilt and iniquities; the chastisement [needful to obtain] peace and well-being for us was upon Him, and with the stripes [that wounded] Him we are healed and made whole.

ISAIAH 53:3-5
(Amplified Bible)

15 And let the peace (soul harmony which comes) from Christ rule (act as umpire continually) in your hearts [deciding and settling with finality all questions that arise in your minds, in that peaceful state] to which as [members of Christ's] one body you were also called [to live]. And be thankful (appreciative), [giving praise to God always].

16 Let the word [spoken by] Christ (the Messiah) have its home [in your hearts and minds] and dwell in you in [all its] richness, as you teach and admonish and train one another in all insight and intelligence and wisdom [in spiritual things, and as you sing] psalms and hymns and spiritual songs, making melody to God with [His] grace in your hearts.

17 And whatever you do [no matter what it is] in word or deed, do everything in the name of the Lord Jesus and in [dependence upon] His Person, giving praise to God the Father through Him.

COLOSSIANS 3:15-17
(Amplified Bible)

14-19 My response is to get down on my knees

before the Father, this magnificent Father who parcels out all heaven and earth. I ask him to strengthen you by his Spirit—not a brute strength but a glorious inner strength—that Christ will live in you as you open the door and invite him in. And I ask him that with both feet planted firmly on love, you'll be able to take in with all followers of Jesus the extravagant dimensions of Christ's love. Reach out and experience the breadth! Test its length! Plumb the depths! Rise to the heights! Live full lives, full in the fullness of God.

20-21 God can do anything, you know—far more than you could ever imagine or guess or request in your wildest dreams! He does it not by pushing us around but by working within us, his Spirit deeply and gently within us.

EPHESIANS 3:14-21
(The Message Bible)

9-12 Be assured that from the first day we heard of you, we haven't stopped praying for you, asking God to give you wise minds and spirits attuned to his will, and so acquire a thorough understanding of the ways in which God works. We pray that you'll live well for the Master, making him proud of you as you work hard in his orchard. As you learn more and more how God works, you will learn how to do your work. We pray that you'll have the strength to stick it out over the long haul—not the grim strength of gritting your teeth but the glory-strength God gives. It is strength that endures the unendurable and spills over into joy, thanking the Father who makes us strong enough to take part in everything bright and beautiful that he has for us.

13-14 God rescued us from dead-end alleys and dark dungeons. He's set us up in the kingdom of the Son he loves so much, the Son who got us out of the pit we were in, got rid of the sins we were doomed to keep repeating.

COLOSSIANS 1:9-14
(The Message Bible)

14-16 Bless your enemies; no cursing under your breath. Laugh with your happy friends when they're happy; share tears when they're down. Get along with each other; don't be stuck-up. Make friends with nobodies; don't be the great somebody.

17-19 Don't hit back; discover beauty in everyone. If you've got it in you, get along with everybody. Don't insist on getting even; that's not for you to do. "I'll do the judging," says God. "I'll take care of it."

20-21 Our Scriptures tell us that if you see your enemy hungry, go buy that person lunch, or if he's thirsty, get him a drink. Your generosity will surprise him with goodness. Don't let evil get the best of you; get the best of evil by doing good.

ROMANS 12:14-21
(The Message Bible)

15-19 That's why, when I heard of the solid trust you have in the Master Jesus and your outpouring of love to all the followers of Jesus, I couldn't stop thanking God for you—every time I prayed, I'd think of you and give thanks. But I do more than thank. I ask—ask the God of our Master, Jesus Christ, the God of glory—to make you intelligent and discerning in knowing him personally, your eyes focused and clear, so that you can see exactly what it is he is calling you to do, grasp the immensity of this glorious way of life he has for his followers, oh, the utter extravagance of his work in us who trust him—endless energy, boundless strength!

20-23 All this energy issues from Christ: God raised him from death and set him on a throne in deep heaven, in charge of running the universe, everything from galaxies to governments, no name and no power exempt from his rule. And not just for the time being, but forever. He is in charge of it all, has the final word on everything. At the center of all this, Christ rules the church. The church, you see, is not peripheral to the world; the world is peripheral to the church. The church is Christ's body, in which he speaks and acts, by which he fills everything with his presence.

EPHESIANS 1:15-23
(The Message Bible)

32 He who did not withhold or spare [even] His own Son but gave Him up for us all, will He not also with Him freely and graciously give us all [other] things?

33 Who shall bring any charge against God's elect [when it is] God Who justifies [that is, Who puts us in right relation to Himself? Who shall come forward and accuse or impeach those whom God has chosen? Will God, Who acquits us?]

34 Who is there to condemn [us]? Will Christ Jesus (the Messiah), Who died, or rather Who was raised from the dead, Who is at the right hand of God actually pleading as He intercedes for us?

35 Who shall ever separate us from Christ's love? Shall suffering and affliction and tribulation? Or calamity and distress? Or persecution or hunger or destitution or peril or sword?

ROMANS 8:32-35
(Amplified Bible)

But God demonstrates his own love for us in this: While we were still sinners, Christ died for us.

ROMANS 5:8
(New International Version)

Though the mountains be shaken and the hills be removed, yet my unfailing love for you will not be shaken nor my covenant of peace be removed," says the LORD, Who has compassion on you.

ISAIAH 54:10
(New International Version)

This fulfilled the word of the Lord through the prophet Isaiah, who said, "He took our sicknesses and removed our diseases."

MATTHEW 8:17
(New Living Translation)

Jesus Christ (the Messiah) is [always] the same, yesterday, today, [yes] and forever (to the ages).

HEBREWS 13:8
(Amplified Bible)

And you know that God anointed Jesus of Nazareth with the Holy Spirit and with power. Then Jesus went around doing good and healing all who were oppressed by the devil, for God was with him.

ACTS 10:38
(New Living Translation)

What shall we say about such wonderful things as these? If God is for us, who can ever be against us?

ROMANS 8:31
(New Living Translation)

And how can men [be expected to] preach unless they are sent? As it is written, how beautiful are the feet of those who bring glad tidings! [How welcome is the coming of those who preach the good news of His good things!] [Isaiah 52:7]

ROMANS 10:15
(Amplified Bible)

10 For as the rain and snow come down from the heavens, and return not there again, but water the

earth and make it bring forth and sprout, that it may give seed to the sower and bread to the eater, [2 Corinthians 9:10]

11 So shall My word be that goes forth out of My mouth: it shall not return to Me void [without producing any effect, useless], but it shall accomplish that which I please and purpose, and it shall prosper in the thing for which I sent it.

ISAIAH 55:10-11
(Amplified Bible)

Behold, I am the Lord, the God of all flesh; is there anything too hard for Me?

JEREMIAH 32:27
(Amplified Bible)

For with God nothing shall be impossible.

LUKE 1:37
(King James Bible)

I will give you the keys of the kingdom of heaven; and whatever you bind (declare to be improper and unlawful) on earth must be what is already bound in heaven; and whatever you loose (declare lawful) on earth must be what is already loosed in heaven. [Isaiah 22:22]

MATTHEW 16:19
(Amplified Bible)

Then the LORD said to me, "You have seen well, for I am watching over My word to perform it."

JEREMIAH 1:12
(New American Standard Bible)

For as many as are led by the Spirit of God, they are the sons of God.

ROMANS 8:14
(King James Version)

I pray that God, the source of hope, will fill you

completely with joy and peace because you trust in him. Then you will overflow with confident hope through the power of the Holy Spirit.

ROMANS 15:13
(New Living Translation)

Such hope never disappoints or deludes or shames us, for God's love has been poured out in our hearts through the Holy Spirit Who has been given to us.

ROMANS 5:5
(Amplified Bible)

"I, the LORD, never change."

MALACHI 3:6
(God's Word Translation)

6 Do not fret or have any anxiety about anything, but in every circumstance and in everything, by prayer and petition (definite requests), with thanksgiving, continue to make your wants known to God.

7 And God's peace [shall be yours, that tranquil state of a soul assured of its salvation through Christ, and so fearing nothing from God and being content with its earthly lot of whatever sort that is, that peace] which transcends all understanding shall garrison and mount guard over your hearts and minds in Christ Jesus.

PHILIPPIANS 4:6-7
(Amplified Bible)

16 The Spirit Himself [thus] testifies together with our own spirit, [assuring us] that we are children of God.

17 And if we are [His] children, then we are [His] heirs also: heirs of God and fellow heirs with Christ [sharing His inheritance with Him]; only we must share His suffering if we are to share His glory.

18 [But what of that?] For I consider that the sufferings of this present time (this present life) are not worth being compared with the glory that is about to be revealed to us and in us and for us and conferred on us!

ROMANS 8:16-18
(Amplified Bible)

15 We have a chief priest who is able to sympathize with our weaknesses. He was tempted in every way that we are, but he didn't sin.

16 So we can go confidently to the throne of God's kindness to receive mercy and find kindness, which will help us at the right time.

HEBREWS 4:15-16
(God's Word Translation)

1 Therefore, since we are justified (acquitted, declared righteous, and given a right standing with God) through faith, let us [grasp the fact that we] have [the peace of reconciliation to hold and to enjoy] peace with God through our Lord Jesus Christ (the Messiah, the Anointed One).

2 Through Him also we have [our] access (entrance, introduction) by faith into this grace (state of God's favor) in which we [firmly and safely] stand. And let

us rejoice and exult in our hope of experiencing and enjoying the glory of God.

ROMANS 5:1-2
(Amplified Bible)

33 But seek (aim at and strive after) first of all His kingdom and His righteousness (His way of doing and being right), and then all these things taken together will be given you besides.

34 So do not worry or be anxious about tomorrow, for tomorrow will have worries and anxieties of its own. Sufficient for each day is its own trouble.

MATTHEW 6:33-34
(Amplified Bible)

Sin is no longer your master, for you no longer live under the requirements of the law. Instead, you live under the freedom of God's grace.

ROMANS 6:14
(New Living Translation)

For our sake He made Christ [virtually] to be sin Who knew no sin, so that in and through Him we might become [endued with, viewed as being in, and examples of] the righteousness of God [what we ought to be, approved and acceptable and in right relationship with Him, by His goodness].

2 CORINTHIANS 5:21
(Amplified Bible)

1 Therefore, [there is] now no condemnation (no adjudging guilty of wrong) for those who are in Christ Jesus, who live [and] walk not after the dictates of the flesh, but after the dictates of the Spirit. [John 3:18]

2 For the law of the Spirit of life [which is] in Christ Jesus [the law of our new being] has freed me from the law of sin and of death.

ROMANS 8:1-2
(Amplified Bible)

And Christ lives within you, so even though your

body will die because of sin, the Spirit gives you life because you have been made right with God.

ROMANS 8:10
(New Living Translation)

For the sin of this one man, Adam, caused death to rule over many. But even greater is God's wonderful grace and his gift of righteousness, for all who receive it will live in triumph over sin and death through this one man, Jesus Christ.

ROMANS 5:17
(New Living Translation)

The wicked run away when no one is chasing them, but the godly are as bold as lions.

PROVERBS 28:1
(New Living Translation)

19 Therefore, brethren, since we have full freedom and confidence to enter into the [Holy of] Holies [by

the power and virtue] in the blood of Jesus,

20 By this fresh (new) and living way which He initiated and dedicated and opened for us through the separating curtain (veil of the Holy of Holies), that is, through His flesh,

21 And since we have [such] a great and wonderful and noble Priest [Who rules] over the house of God,

22 Let us all come forward and draw near with true (honest and sincere) hearts in unqualified assurance and absolute conviction engendered by faith (by that leaning of the entire human personality on God in absolute trust and confidence in His power, wisdom, and goodness), having our hearts sprinkled and purified from a guilty (evil) conscience and our bodies cleansed with pure water.

23 So let us seize and hold fast and retain without wavering the hope we cherish and confess and our acknowledgement of it, for He Who promised is reliable (sure) and faithful to His word.

24 And let us consider and give attentive, continuous care to watching over one another, studying how we

may stir up (stimulate and incite) to love and helpful deeds and noble activities,

25 Not forsaking or neglecting to assemble together [as believers], as is the habit of some people, but admonishing (warning, urging, and encouraging) one another, and all the more faithfully as you see the day approaching.

HEBREWS 10:19-25
(Amplified Bible)

17 So it is evident that it was essential that He be made like His brethren in every respect, in order that He might become a merciful (sympathetic) and faithful High Priest in the things related to God, to make atonement and propitiation for the people's sins.

18 For because He Himself [in His humanity] has suffered in being tempted (tested and tried), He is able [immediately] to run to the cry of (assist, relieve) those who are being tempted and tested and tried [and who therefore are being exposed to suffering].

HEBREWS 2:17-18
(Amplified Bible)

17 [After all] the kingdom of God is not a matter of [getting the] food and drink [one likes], but instead it is righteousness (that state which makes a person acceptable to God) and [heart] peace and joy in the Holy Spirit.

18 He who serves Christ in this way is acceptable and pleasing to God and is approved by men.

19 So let us then definitely aim for and eagerly pursue what makes for harmony and for mutual up building (edification and development) of one another.

ROMANS 14:17-19
(Amplified Bible)

17 But the wisdom from above is first of all pure. It is also peace loving, gentle at all times, and willing to yield to others. It is full of mercy and good deeds. It shows no favoritism and is always sincere.

18 And those who are peacemakers will plant seeds of peace and reap a harvest of righteousness.

JAMES 3:17-18
(New Living Translation)

Try to live peacefully with everyone, and try to live holy lives, because if you don't, you will not see the Lord.

HEBREWS 12:14
(God's Word Translation)

When you enter a home, greet the family, 'Peace.' If your greeting is received, then it's a good place to stay. But if it's not received, take it back and get out. Don't impose yourself.

LUKE 10:5-6
(The Message Bible)

12 May the Lord greatly increase your love for each other and for all people, just as we love you.

13 Then your hearts will be strong, blameless, and holy in the presence of God, who is our Father, when our Lord Jesus appears with all his saints.

1 THESSALONIANS 3:12-13
(International Standard Version)

1 So by whatever [appeal to you there is in our mutual dwelling in Christ, by whatever] strengthening and consoling and encouraging [our relationship] in Him [affords], by whatever persuasive incentive there is in love, by whatever participation in the [Holy] Spirit [we share], and by whatever depth of affection and compassionate sympathy,

2 Fill up and complete my joy by living in harmony and being of the same mind and one in purpose, having the same love, being in full accord and of one harmonious mind and intention.

3 Do nothing from factional motives [through contentiousness, strife, selfishness, or for unworthy ends] or prompted by conceit and empty arrogance. Instead, in the true spirit of humility (lowliness of mind) let each regard the others as better than and

superior to himself [thinking more highly of one another than you do of yourselves].

4 Let each of you esteem and look upon and be concerned for not [merely] his own interests, but also each for the interests of others.

5 Let this same attitude and purpose and [humble] mind be in you which was in Christ Jesus: [Let Him be your example in humility:]

PHILIPPIANS 2:1-5
(Amplified Bible)

You have not for the second time acquired the consciousness of being--a consciousness which fills you with terror. But you have acquired a deep inward conviction of having been adopted as sons--a conviction which prompts us to cry aloud, "Abba! Our Father!"

ROMANS 8:15
(Weymouth New Testament)

Blessed (enjoying enviable happiness, spiritually prosperous—with life-joy and satisfaction in God's favor and salvation, regardless of their outward conditions) are the makers and maintainers of peace, for they shall be called the sons of God!

MATTHEW 5:9
(Amplified Bible)

For God is not the author of confusion, but of peace, as in all churches of the saints.

1 CORINTHIANS 14:33
(King James 2000 Bible)

3 Not only so, but we also glory in our sufferings, because we know that suffering produces perseverance;

4 perseverance, character; and character, hope.

5 And hope does not put us to shame, because God's love has been poured out into our hearts through the Holy Spirit, who has been given to us

ROMANS 5:3-5
(New International Version)

10 But it is The God of grace who has called us to his eternal glory by Yeshua The Messiah, who gives us, while we shall endure these small afflictions, to be empowered, confirmed and established in him to eternity;

11 To him is the glory, the dominion and the honor to the eternity of eternities. Amen.

1 PETER 5:10-11
(Aramaic Bible in Plain English)

16 "This is the covenant I will make with them after that time, says the Lord. I will put my laws in their hearts, and I will write them on their minds."

17 Then he adds: "Their sins and lawless acts I will remember no more."

HEBREWS 10:16-17
(New International Version)

Christ suffered for our sins once for all time. He never sinned, but he died for sinners to bring you safely home to God. He suffered physical death, but he was raised to life in the Spirit.

1 PETER 3:18
(New Living Translation)

20 The God of peace brought the great shepherd of the sheep, our Lord Jesus, back to life through the blood of an eternal promise.

21 May this God of peace prepare you to do every good thing he wants. May he work in us through Jesus Christ to do what is pleasing to him. Glory belongs to Jesus Christ forever. Amen.

HEBREWS 13:20-21
(God's Word Translation)

8 He will keep you strong to the end so that you will be free from all blame on the day when our Lord Jesus Christ returns.

9 God will do this, for he is faithful to do what he says, and he has invited you into partnership with his Son, Jesus Christ our Lord.

1 CORINTHIANS 1:8-9
(New Living Translation)

23 But The God of peace shall make all of you perfectly holy and shall keep your whole spirit, soul and body without fault for the arrival of our Lord Yeshua The Messiah.

24 Faithful is he who has called you; it is he who shall perform it.

1 THESSALONIANS 5:23-24
(Aramaic Bible in Plain English)

"Everyone's going through a refining fire sooner or later, but you'll be well-preserved, protected from the eternal flames. Be preservatives yourselves. Preserve the peace."

MARK 9:50

(The Message Bible)

A person may plan his own journey, but the LORD directs his steps.

PROVERBS 16:9
(God's Word Translation)

57 But thank God! He gives us victory over sin and death through our Lord Jesus Christ.

58 So, my dear brothers and sisters, be strong and immovable. Always work enthusiastically for the Lord, for you know that nothing you do for the Lord is ever useless.

1 CORINTHIANS 15:57-58
(New Living Translation)

Dear friend, I know that you are spiritually well. I pray that you're doing well in every other way and that you're healthy.

3 JOHN 1:2
(God's Word Translation)

4 I always thank God for you because Christ Jesus has shown you God's good will.

5 Through Christ Jesus you have become rich in every way-in speech and knowledge of every kind.

6 Our message about Christ has been verified among you.

7 Therefore, you don't lack any gift as you wait eagerly for our Lord Jesus Christ
to be revealed.

1 CORINTHIANS 1:4-7
(God's Word Translation)

But I thank God, who always leads us in victory because of Christ. Wherever we go, God uses us to make clear what it means to know Christ.
It's like a fragrance that fills the air.

2 CORINTHIANS 2:14
(God's Word Translation)

19-20 And so while there has never been any question about your honesty in these matters—I couldn't be more proud of you! I want you also to be smart, making sure every "good" thing is the real thing. Don't be gullible in regard to smooth-talking evil. Stay alert like this, and before you know it the God of peace will come down on Satan with both feet, stomping him into the dirt. Enjoy the best of Jesus!

ROMANS 16:20
(The Message Bible)

Love never does anything that is harmful to a neighbor. Therefore, love fulfills Moses' Teachings.

ROMANS 13:10
(God's Word Translation)

It is foolish to belittle one's neighbor; a sensible

person keeps quiet.

PROVERBS 11:12
(New Living Translation)

Stay away from lusts which tempt young people. Pursue what has God's approval. Pursue faith, love, and peace together with those who worship the Lord with a pure heart.

2 TIMOTHY 2:22
(God's Word Translation)

22 But the Holy Spirit produces this kind of fruit in our lives: love, joy, peace, patience, kindness, goodness, faithfulness,

23 gentleness, and self-control. There is no law against these things!

GALATIANS 5:22-23
(New Living Translation)

8 Finally, all of you be harmonious, sympathetic,

affectionate, compassionate, and humble.

9 Do not return evil for evil or insult for insult, but instead bless others because you were called to inherit a blessing.

10 For the one who wants to love life and see good days must keep his tongue from evil and his lips from uttering deceit.

11 And he must turn away from evil and do good; he must seek peace and pursue it.

12 For the eyes of the Lord are upon the righteous and his ears are open to their prayer. But the Lord's face is against those who do evil.

13 For who is going to harm you if you are devoted to what is good?

1 PETER 3:8-13
(New English Translation Bible)

Finally, brethren, farewell (rejoice)! Be strengthened (perfected, completed, made what you ought to be); be encouraged and consoled and comforted; be of the same [agreeable] mind one with another; live in peace, and [then] the God of love [Who is the Source of affection, goodwill, love, and benevolence toward men] and the Author and
Promoter of peace will be with you.

2 CORINTHIANS 13:11
(Amplified Bible)

Conclusion

Thank you again for purchasing this book!

I hope this book has helped you find comfort for your soul in a time of need.

The next step is to enjoy your new and brighter days.

Thank you for your time. I wish you the best of luck!

Chris Adkins

http://www.livingabrightlifenow.com

Check Out My Other Books On Amazon

If you are interested, you will find other 'Religion & Spirituality' books that are popular on Amazon and Kindle as well. Simply copy and paste the book title into the search bar on Amazon dot Com. Alternatively, you can visit my author page on Amazon to see other work done by me.

https://www.amazon.com/author/cadkins

The Names Of God From A To Z Explained: Exploring God's Character With 1000+ Names Of God And Their Meanings ~ By Chris Adkins

List Of 'I AM' Affirmations ~ By Chris Adkins

Healing Scriptures From Genesis To Revelation: 300 Healing Bible Verses On The Proven Healing Promises

From God's Word ~ By Chris Adkins

Chronicles Of The Kings Of Israel And Judah: Timeline And List Of The Kings Of Israel In Order ~ By Chris Adkins

The Genealogy Of Jesus In The Bible: A Chronological List Of The Genealogy Of Jesus Through Mary ~ By Chris Adkins

Healing Scriptures For A Broken Heart: Experience Emotional Healing And Healing The Wounds Of The Past ~ By Chris Adkins

Grieving A Loss: Scriptures On Grief Recovery And Coping With Grief And Loss ~ By Chris Adkins

Forgiven: Scriptures On Forgiveness And Proven

Second Chances ~ By Chris Adkins

Life Or Death: Salvation By Grace Scriptures And Holy Spirit Scriptures To Live By ~ By Chris Adkins